# a book you still hide

dedicated to

all who have fed me, bought me cigarettes, bought me clothes, bought me books, and housed me (and continue to) while I make no money in art and poetry. this is also for those who drank coffee with me at cafes while I wrote, drank beer with me at bars while listening to me ramble about Bukowski, and to all those people who unwillingly let me people watch you for inspiration

# Table of Contents

| | |
|---|---|
| at the airport | 4 |
| The Jazz Age | 5 |
| the herd | 6 |
| 16th and Locust | 7 |
| 60 degrees | 8 |
| un cafe | 9 |
| City | 10 |
| w-r-r-i-i-g-t-h-e-t | 11 |
| Home | 12 |
| greener | 13 |
| Bukowski | 14 |
| sunday morning poems | 15 |
| the new place | 16 |
| Note to Self | 17 |
| and I stare at her | 18 |
| death of a salesman | 19 |
| a book you still hide | 20 |
| one for two | 21 |
| magnanimous | 23 |
| hands of a god | 24 |
| that simple | 25 |
| ballet | 26 |
| Power | 27 |
| Born Too Late | 28 |
| My Masterpiece | 29 |

## at the airport

"I'm a poet."
I tell the bartender,
    the traveler,
    the lady sitting next to me
at the airport.

They say,
"Impressive! Inspiring!
Are you doing readings?
Are you published?"

"Yes.

Bukowski,
Eliot,
Whitman,
Cohen,
Dylan,
Cummings,
Ginsberg,
Masso.

I'm a poet."

I say my line,
look down at my drink,
sigh,
and then my stomach begins to hurt,

because it always hurts when I lie.

## The Jazz Age

O how I love the peace
on the days with dark clouds
no sun
temperature a bit chilly
enough for a jacket
and a heater
slightly burning the hair
on my arms
and
I read
a book by Hemingway
or Fitzgerald
something olde
something classy
something about
writers speaking with writers
and wearing suits
and drinking cocktails
and smoking cigarettes
and the women
watch them speak
of art in awe
and a few even understand
and on these days I
trade my beer
for coffee or even
hot chocolate
and I read
and I read
and I think of love
and act it out
in my head
and I think not
of my appearance
of my money
of my schedule
and think only of
this world
that I so long
to live in

## The herd

it was a tuesday
at 5:45 pm
and I saw an opening

it was two lanes to my right
and I was boxed in
by a ford in front of me
      and
by a toyota to the right of me

I couldn't get to it

I saw a car
zoom in between lanes
at 85 mph
and I saw him
get into the opening
and he zoomed even faster
and he zoomed until he was gone
and I felt like applauding
and I felt like shouting
and I was filled with happiness

at least one of us
broke free

## 16th and Locust

you get numb

to
the fights
the beatings
the needles in arms
the sniffing
the vomit under your seat
on the train

you get numb

so
you don't call the cops
you keep walking forward
you don't make eye contact
you keep your head down
you lift your legs
and continue riding

keep reading your paperback
and
keep your feet up

you
will get home
eventually

## 60 Degrees

it has been a much
too dead stop
    winter
but today
I am outside
with my typewriter
with my cigar
with my t-shirt
with my beer
and I am watching
the dogs run around
the yard
panting
and barking
and happy

and I haven't sent
a single publisher
anything this
whole winter
and today that will change
and my pockets
will feel heavier
and I will get
a summer body
and a broken
fall

and spring can go
fuck itself

and I think that
life is beautiful
but I think it
with caution
for tomorrow
I have to work
and I will
once again
pray for the
snow

**un cafè**

it's 70 degrees out
and I have an article due
and a book due
tonight
and I stare at my papers
then look outside
then think
of Bourdain

so I gather my papers
and I get in my car
and drive to a bar
with the windows open
and I spread my papers
across the bar
and order a beer
and a sweet tea
and I write
my article
my book
and some poems
about writing
with beer
music
and a breeze

and I take in the people
around me
and write a few more
poems

and for a day
I pretend I am a writer

# City

"Show me the city." I said to her.
She smiled and grabbed my hand.
"I'm ready to be spontaneous."
"I'm the one to be spontaneous with." she winked.

I bought a ukulele, just for the hell of it,
at an old Spanish music store.
What would I do if the strings broke?
I didn't care.

I didn't want to fly back home with it.
I also didn't want to leave it for her.
She already had one.
I'll guess I'll have to live here

because of the ukulele - not her.

**w-r-r-i-i-g-t-h-e-t**

I'm supposed to write, right?
write when I want to write
write when I don't want to write
write when I'm not alright
write when I am alright
write right now
right now I should write
write about right now
write about her being right
write about her not being right
write about me being right
write about no one being right
write about writing
right on
write on
right?
write?
———>

**Home**

She reads on the train
that allows her to roam.
Her empathy keeps her going
as she stays away from home.

She has a collection of photos
she's taken from place to place.
She writes for them and feels their pain
as she studies every face.

She's the independent romantic,
    the holder of the key.
She's the tormented spirit,
    the Greek tragedy.

Her face shines in my mind sometimes
as I lay alone in bed.
I still read the letters you sent me,
but I don't forgive what you said.

How could I be at peace with you
leaving me here unstable?
You can see "Confidence" inked on my skin
as a warning label.

I know you have demons to outrun.
I know you have shit to figure out.
I'm just not the one you should have left, babe.
I'm the home you dream about.

**greener**

making love in a loft
nothing but glass
so the world can watch

making love while
the city eats and shits
and drinks and sweats

making love while
they drive to appointments
and drive to funerals

making love while
they work
and I do not

making love
better than ever
in a new place

nothing brings about
great love making
like traveling

but heed the warning

it will end when you
go back home

## Bukowski

Bukowski wrote
"what matters most is
how well you
walk through the
fire."

he believed that –
that's why he didn't kill himself

he was not a hypocrite –
an exaggerator
or actor,
yes,
but not a hypocrite

he believed that
and it hurts me

it hurts me
because I do not do well with fire

I am a coward –
just like Bukowski

he hated cowards
so he hated himself
and he'd hate me

Bukowski didn't walk well
through the fire
he wasn't talking about himself
when he wrote that line
he was talking about
the people he idolized
and

my idol
wouldn't
idolize me

## sunday morning poems

there's a coffee mug
half full
on my left
my ashtray
to my right
and center
is my notebook
and pen

I write some sunday morning
poems
and call my wife over
"hey, babe,
what do you think?"
and she doesn't give an answer
she just makes sarcastic jokes
like
"what does this mean, poet?"
and
"is this about you being homosexual?"

later
the mail comes
and the magazine writes
and says
"thank you for sending us
your poems,
but they do not fit
our style."

my wife reads the letter
and says
"they are stupid.
I don't understand
how your stuff doesn't sell."

I've learned
that
she thinks I am a good artist

she just hints at it
in her own poetic way

**the new place**

in a grey town
I long for
a conversation in a cheap room
and I think that would cure
everything
a
good
conversation in a cheap room
about cummings, plath,
pollock, the death of poetry,
and the birth
of cubic zirconium hearts

fill my room
with red laughter,
for
rent is higher than it should be
(how I long for Buk's
3 and a half dollar a week room)
and this town is no good
for Art,

give me what I lack
and the price of rent
may be easier to swallow
   like a watered down vodka
and the crows peck my books
and my wallet and my cats

and the crows peck my books
and my wallet and my cats

**Note to Self**

I've learned
that if I write
while I'm
upset
depressed
angry
scared
or any other
emotion

my poems turn out
too angst-y
too childish
too bitch-y
too fake
or any other
synonym for shit

I have to journal
my immature feelings
and go back to them
when I am neutral
whatever the hell
neutral is

write drunk edit sober
only applies to being
legitimately drunk

not drunk on emotion

I must write about feeling
after I've felt it
instead of being in the
eye of the hurricane
or else
I sound like a teenager

and no one likes teenagers

**and I stare at her**

I'm sitting on
the loveseat
reading poetry
that is better than mine
and she is across from me
doing a puzzle
under a tiny lamp
and her hair is pulled back
just right
and her face is lit
just right
and I look at her hands
at work
and her finger without a ring
and I stare at her
and I stare at her
and I think about
the ring I bought her
and when I will propose
and how I will afford it
and how I will afford her
and if I can work at all
and if I sleep with all the dogs
and all the cats and all the
things that disrupt
my contentness
but I love her for these things
and wish that she would not
change
but that I would change
and I check my pocket
for loose change
I will need more cigarettes
tonight
and I stare at her again
and I love her so much
that my eyes start to water
and a tear falls on the book

and like a funeral
I cry for poetry and love

## death of a salesman

i know
i know
i do not know
i know
nothing everything
you me him
her
this beer
      this cigarette
   this pornography
  this money i am
spending
to forget
   to remember
you me
them
her
                it

i love it
i love this
i love all this
yet i curse you
    for your emotions
  cause they affect
      mine
and make me
do this love this
love you
love you dearly
love you truly
love you love me
please love me
please don't forget me
     don't forget me

come to bed
i promise
      promise?

come to bed

**a book you still hide**

a story,
a story,
tell me a story!

a fox and a cat
a moth and a fire
a bear eats my arm
a hitman for hire

a life surely wasted
a rat in my trap
a balloon up too high
a line on your map

a song that you sing
a gun in the dark
a plane coming down
a love without spark

a gift to the homeless
a present for me
a shallow wet pool
a fear you can see

a new way to die
a hill full of pride
a zoo without you
a book you still hide

a god in the sky
a pole in the ground
a juggler and mime
a herd without sound

a thief in the night
a room smells of grape
a vase shatters now
a black cassette tape

a steel bar in front
a grown man is crying
a pastor spills ink
a lion is dying

**one for two**

I do nothing
in poetry,
not art,
without meaning

each line is under another
next to another
split for a reason

each word is under another
next to another
lowercase for a reason

it is a form of painting
visual as much as
verbal
and a word spaced
barely to
the left
      or
            under
or    ALonE
can change
the enjoyment
or meaning
for the reader
  and writer

even when I post
these poems
on    INSTAGRAM (in 2018)
they are black text
      white background
times new roman
11pt font    like
an application for
a job interview
- which I infer this is
but my poems are
written and posted
like this for a reason

I beg the reader
to view my work
as well thought out and
artistic -

at least visually

because the same
cannot always be said
for the
        words.

**magnanimous**

we decided to take a nap
and I was the first one
awake
and I noticed
a moon
and stars
a full bladder
and a headache
from lack of cheap food
and too much cheap alcohol

her head
was pinning down
my arm
so
I had to decide
between letting her sleep
or
potentially waking her up

I looked at her face
         her hair
            her chest

and
I let her sleep

since she has to
go to work

and I do not

## hands of a god

there's something maturing
about fixing your own tire

jacking up the car
putting your body weight
behind each turn
of the lugs
kicking the tire off
carrying the sonofabitch
to the nearest mechanic
walking in with the tire
on your shoulder
and your chest held high
like it's a trophy
smoking cigarettes as you wait
admiring the cuts and dirt
on your hands
and repeating the process
in the opposite order

you take in the world
you hear the silence
you alone

accomplishing this task
is like an awakening
of the spirit
you realize how hard
and easy life is

there's a metaphor
in changing a tire

I just don't know what it is

**that simple**

wake up
take a piss
go to the cupboard
and find that there is no coffee
take out a cigarette
and walk outside
and the landlord is there
screaming and flailing
and yelling and spitting
walk past him
to the car
and it won't start
and the wife won't answer
your phone call
because she hates your face
and the bar is walking distance
and you walk
and you arrive
and you drink
and you spend
the last fifty dollars
on booze
instead of a battery

and everyone's advice is
Get. A. Job.

**ballet**

I got yelled at
for buying a chair
because I am
out of work again
"but that is what
credit cards are for",
I said,
"and I needed a chair"
and she told me to get a job
one that can buy a bigger house
and more dinners
cooked by the best
and more clothes that
the one percent wear
and I stared forward
and told her that there
are no careers left
and even if there were
that I don't want them
and that I would be wasted
on them
and she left
and slammed the door
and I sipped my beer
and continued watching
professional wrestling -
two sweaty guys
in a ballet of art and emotion -
and they are not being
wasted by performing

and then I wrote this poem
and I once again
worked for free

**Power**

He had too much empathy,
and not enough power,
to play God with others,
so he played God on himself.

## Born too late

A publisher wrote back to me
"Your work is too Bukowski.
I don't like Bukowski."

What he wanted to write was
"Your work won't sell.
I need money."

Maybe he's right.
Maybe it won't sell,
but at least it has soul.

I wrote back
"I understand.
Thanks for reading."

What I wanted to write was
"You make soulless poets rich.
Good writing isn't just metaphors."

I may sound like Bukowski,
but I'm not faking my art,

he was just born first.

## My Masterpiece

My funeral will be my last
                        artistic masterpiece.
Watch what I can make you feel.

**Acknowledgements**

"Home"
"My Masterpiece"
"Power"
were first published by *Spillwords Press*.

"City"
was first published by *Heavenly Flower Publishing/Bindweed Magazine*.

"at the airport"
"Bukowski"
were first published by *Duane's PoeTree*

www.ingramcontent.com/pod-product-compliance
Lightning Source LLC
Chambersburg PA
CBHW022000290426
44108CB00012B/1158